MEET ME AT THE CROSS:
ONE WOMAN'S TESTIMONY

By

Pastor Jonita L. (Jay) Johnson

*Dedicated to All my children,
and all those who have hung the
precious name of mom on me.*

*Craig, Edward, Matthew, Loren,
Chad, Cornelius, LaMeaka,
and my baby girl, Denita*

*Big Michael wherever you are may
the Lord's blessings
be with you, Lil' Michael,
thank you for
being a son to me.
Myzell,
You'll always hold a
special place in my heart.*

*Legacies are our inherited responsibilities,
and hopefully pleasures to pass from
one generation to another. Mine to you,
TRUST in the Lord. Turn all situations
over to God our Father, and BELIEVE
that His Holy and Right will for you
will always be done.
Jesus said He would NEVER leave us or forsake
us.*

I Love You – Always & Forever,

MOM

ACKNOWLEDGEMENTS

This work would have never been completed if not for the Holy Spirit giving me the courage to tell all (mostly), and special people the Lord places in my life. This is the second writing of this. When it was first published in 1977, Reverend Russell Morrow did the printing through his publishing company New Generation Ministries. You can still view some of my writings, and many of his sermons by going to www.Newgenmin.org. Rev. Morrow and his family are still very much a part of my support group.

My Pastor here in Bellingham, Pastor Baron Miller of Roosevelt Community Church, who coined the motto for Roosevelt Church, In For and With the Community. He is a visionary that follows through. I thank Rev. Kenneth Ransfer at Mt. Baker Baptist Church in Seattle, Washington, for directing me to Rev. Smith at Allen Temple in Oakland. I learned so much while a member of Allen Temple about urban ministry. Allen Temple is a great example of Christ in the community.

As a loner, there are a few sista's who would not let me alone, and I'm so blessed to have them in my life; Barbara Mines-Jones in Oakland, Marion Redwood and Rita Coleman Columbus, Ms, Two women who have totally been here for me since I moved to Bellingham are Desiree Edwards and Renee Walrod. The editing would not have gotten done without another lady I can add to my sista' list, Jo Collinge. Thank you so much.

There are two other women in my life that have been with me, supported me, fussed at me, ignored at times, but always their love has been with me. There is a song that says, Somebody Prayed For Me this they did, even when I didn't want their prayers. These two women NEVER stopped loving me or believing in me; Darlene Brewer, my mom and Frieda Simmons, my grandmother. They are the strongest, givenest, and greatest Christian women I know.

I love you all - Thank You

INTRODUCTION:

If you are taking the time to read this book, most likely you are a person with a need. You may have been and still are addicted to a drug or alcohol. You may be a victim of incest, rape, spousal abuse, or domestic violence in whatever form it takes affect upon a person. Maybe you're an abuser or a thief. Maybe you have killed someone or caused serious injury. You might even be broke, busted and just downright disgusted with this thing called life, and everyone and everything in it. Perhaps you're even thinking of suicide. Take it from one who's tried, been there, and done that (several times), it's not the better or the easiest way.

You might be a parent worried about a child, or a child worried about a parent. Whatever your situation, know now that no one EVER cared more about you than the man —Jesus, Your Son praise for the difference that is being made in our lives today. AMEN

Marriage, parenting, and sometimes just living are the hardest jobs in the world. Yes, some of us have to make a commitment just to live one day at a time. It is a commitment that requires hard work; and it doesn't go unrewarded. Before entering this commitment, it would be wise if we really know who we are, and what baggage we are carrying around with us. Just what is it we are taking into our relationships, marriages

and parenting experiences? What issues
within us can be discarded? What values can
we add, build on, or throw away? What do we
really want from life, our relationships
with others, what do we want from God?

   **At this point, you might have many
questions, and no answers – that's
okay. Without questions we would
never receive answers.**

MY BACKGROUND

At the time of the first writing of this I was 51 years old. I'm 60, and feelin' great. As far as the update on this book, the story is the same, but some things have happened. One of the things that happened is a misunderstanding within my family. Beside Jesus, my mom and grandmother are my life supports. The two of them are the inspiration of most things that I have achieved and do. So no part of this book is accusing them of anything other than loving me. Life happens, and we learn to deal with it. Now we proceed.

I was raised in the teachings of the Baptist church, in a Christian home. So I knew about God, Jesus and all that good stuff. Even though I came from a praying family, it was still a family with many problems. Do you know of a family that doesn't have problems? From the first Adam's family until Jesus comes again, we all will have some dysfunction within our families, some more than others, but dysfunction non-the-less.

I haven't always had a relationship with the Lord. Over the years I've been in and out of the churches. I believed in God, but often found it was too hard to live a Christian life. At one point, I believed I was born bad, born to be a sinner. I had heard from others, and it stayed in my mind that I was the devil's child. I believed that I wasn't and never could be good enough for Jesus to love me, or for God to accept me.

My reasoning was that since I didn't feel accepted by Jesus, I knew He wouldn't and couldn't love me, as bad as I was. So if I wasn't good enough for even God, my maker to love me, how could anything good ever happen to me? How could any man worth anything love me? This one thought, this <u>feeling</u>, was like a persistent mighty undercurrent that directed most of my actions and decisions. I believed that it would take a man to validate who I was as a woman, to be truthful as a valuable human being. Waiting for certain feelings to come can really mess us up. Psalm 145:18, *The Lord is close to all who call upon Him, yes, who call upon Him sincerely.* Jeremiah 23:23, *Am I a God who is only in one place? Asks the LORD…* Acts 17:27, *His purpose in all this was that nations should seek after God and perhaps find Him – though He is not far from any one of us.*

PLEASE don't be deceived while waiting for certain feelings to happen while you seek the Lord or grow in Him. Jesus is with us always. That is a promise to us from Him. If you read no more of this book than the scriptures that I have included – **READ THEM.** It is the Word, His Word, which will draw you to Jesus.

As far back as I can remember, until I was 21 years old, family members and close friends of the family sexually abused me. I was one of the **<u>silent</u>** kids. I never told anyone because of threats that were made. My mom found out about the first person who hurt me, and that was by accident. At eight, I was penetrated and hurt. I didn't know until years later that she did something to stop it. People didn't talk a lot about such things much back in 1953. Unknown to me until years later, when my mom removed me from our home, she went back to confront the person. She wasn't alone, but was accompanied by a gun, what kind I don't know. But she missed him and blew a hole in the wall. He got the idea she wasn't none too happy. I never returned that house. Unknown to her, though she tried to protect me the abuse continued with others.

Some children are made to feel as though they were at fault and caused the abuse to happen. There was a particular person who did this to me, so the abuse continued. The child in me was made to feel responsible for the pain in our family, and if I were to tell I would cause further pain to people I loved. Though it was unfounded, I carried this guilt for years, even through most of my adult life. I thank God that at the age of 21 I found the courage to say, "No more, you will never touch me again." It stopped, but the bitterness, mistrust and confusion about who I really was still existed. This turmoil within still flooded what should have been the peace and quietness of a child's mind.

When children are put into a shameful, guilty silence of endurance they often are targeted by other human predators who have

no condemnation for how deeply they hurt or
who they hurt.

        I never really talked to any adults
during my preteen or young adulthood years.
I still carried the implanted idea of
someone else that I was to blame, that I was
bad. In my early years as a teenager, my mom
and I never really got close; she never
understood my aloofness or my anger. I
learned to use her love for me. I placed
blame on her for sending me away. I was
convinced, by the abuser that she didn't
love me since I ruined her life. I didn't
understand that when she sent me away it was
for my protection, even though it turned out
quite the opposite. I had no idea at eight
years old how hard it was for her to raise a
child alone. I had no idea of the guilt she
suffered because this happened.

        At the age of thirty-one, mom and I
finally sat down together, talked, cried,
and cried some more. There were things she
shared with me about those early years that
we had never before discussed. In the
fifties people were not as open about sexual
abuse as they are now. So she had no idea of
why I was so rebellious and distant from
her, I had NO idea of the depths of her
love. If I had really examined the whole
situation, I could have heard her screaming
the I LOVE YOU'S in all her actions. When I
did return to live with my mom, she made
sure we were in decent, clean apartments. My
mom worked so hard to keep me in decent
clothes. I went through shoes like crazy,
and she tried her best to keep up with my

ever-growing feet. Mom didn't miss work and refused to get on welfare. My mom truly was a woman who walked three to four miles to get to work in Minnesota winters. As I look back, I can see she tried her best to show and give me her love. I didn't know how to receive it, from her or anyone else.

As I grew from childhood to an adult I used to wonder, if I had a sign around my neck that said, "Here I am, **victim** is my name – come get me…," and they did. I hope that someone reading this will realize that people who abuse children know what psychological signs to look for in children. I grew and rebelled, and started looking for **"LOVE."** You know the kind you hear about from records, read about in cheap romance books, and see on the soap operas.

At age 14 I was pregnant. I was determined to keep my baby, and finally have someone to love me. I didn't have a clue that babies learn to love from us, not the other way around. But, with the help of my supportive family of strong women – yes the same family that had so many problems; with their help and prayers, I am now the mom, step-mom, adopted mom of six boys and two girls. And there are three others who have honored me through the years by calling and treating me as mom.

At 15 my grandma took me, and my baby back to Kansas with her. She also had a strong admonition for me. She said, "My getting pregnant this time was a mistake; one anyone could make. The family was there to help me get through school and support me in raising my child. **BUT**, if it happens again, twice is a habit; and I would be on my own". When she spoke like that I knew it was truth. I wasn't anywhere near ready to be on my own and I knew it, so did they.

It has taken many years and at least a million buckets full of tears to get where I can talk openly about my past pain. I've also used counseling services several times along the way. I am not psychologist, just a woman who has experienced some things. And through the power, love and grace of God I have come out whole. My mind is sound, and I am still very much alive. I have been made free to love, forgive, live and give to others.

Through my teenage years, the Lord never left me. His Word seemed to come at me in the strangest places. I think it's that thing we call a conscience, that small quiet voice that tells us when we're wrong or with the wrong people, or in the wrong places. When scripture is put into a child when they are young, the Word of God comes back to protect them and lead them out of would be trouble and temptation. Oh, the joy we could know if we just paid more attention to that quiet voice within.

I call my experience, **<u>THE FOOT OF THE CROSS</u>"** experience. For me things ended and began at the cross. The end was when I began to see sin for what it really is - a killer. At the cross of Jesus Christ I came to understand that my life was not apart from Him. At the cross I began a journey of knowing who I am, what my calling and purpose are in Him. At the cross I learned that knowing who Jesus Christ is, is far different than coming into fellowship with, and growing into an ongoing relationship with the Lord. All these things came into my life at the Cross of Jesus.

<u>**SEATTLE**</u>

The beginning was when the Word of God began to come alive in my life. I went to church occasionally, (which ever one had the best choir) listened to Christian music on Sunday morning radio. Sometimes my conscience really bothered me about some of the things I was doing, the way I was living. Anyway, on this Sunday morning, I'd been cleaning my house, listening to James Cleveland gospel music, and heavily sipping on one of my favorite drinks, Crown Royal. I got tired and laid on the couch, maybe passed out is more truthful.

I dreamed: I was riding down a street that men were working on. They had dug a huge hole in the middle of the street, and were in the process of refilling it. There had been a roadblock, a danger sign, proceed with caution sign. They took it down. I asked if it was safe to drive over it. They said, "yes, it's fine now." As I drove on top of the spot they filled in, my car began to sink. The men began filling it with sand, and I was being completely covered, pulled down into darkness. I was trapped.

I awoke immediately, covered with sweat, and scared. I remembered immediately the scripture about building your house on sand. ***Matthew 7:24-25,…"The rain came down, the streams rose, and the winds blew and beat against that house, and it fell with a great crash."*** Also I couldn't get the song, "On Christ the Solid Rock I Stand, ALL Other ground is SINKING SAND," out of my mind. I

was living my life in quicksand, and I was
sinking. I didn't change clothes (jeans,
sweatshirt & tennis shoes), wash or brush my
teeth to whisk away the taste and smell of
alcohol. I was scared and knew where I must
go. There is a song that says, "Where shall
I go, where shall I go, seeking a refuge for
my soul. Where shall I go, where shall I go?
Where shall I go but to the Lord?"

Many times I had passed by that church
on 23rd & Jackson St., but I never went in,
today I pulled up to the Greater Mount Baker
Missionary Baptist Church on a beautiful,
sunny Sunday morning (during 11:A.M.
service). I was a little bit drunk, and very
much in need of the Lord. As I walked in the
church (in my drunken state), a man by the
name of Deacon Witt (now deceased) saw my
pain, and went to tell the pastor. The late
Reverend W.P. Johnson left his pulpit and
service and ministered right there to my
need. He counseled as a minister and also as
a father. As a father he found out who my
people were (Christian training), and his
all too familiar words, "Girl, you know
better, you know what you need to do, and
where you need to be, how long are you going
to ignore the Lord?"

I did know better. I told Reverend
Johnson that my mind knew the Word, that
Jesus loved me and would forgive me, but my
heart couldn't accept it. No part of me
believed that Jesus could really accept me.
Rev. Johnson said that by faith I needed to
come. "He asked me if I believed the Word of
God, that Jesus was the Son of God, Jesus

died for me, for my sins to be forgiven, and bring me back into relationship with God as my Father." I told him yes, I did believe, but I kept doing the same old things. He told me to trust Jesus to grow me. I didn't understand what growing in the Lord meant.

I began to ask the Lord to reveal His Word to me, to reveal it so I could really understand it. This was just one of many times I had come to the Lord and asked to be shown His Word. I've asked Him time and time again to let me see how it applied to me. What good is reading the Bible if you don't understand it? Did I really want to understand it, or did I want to pick and chose the parts I liked that didn't interfere with what I thought I wanted to do? Yes, many times I had come to this point of seeking, but in my mind I always failed. I had always gone back to the same old routine. No, I really didn't want to know what the Word said if it differed from what I thought I was enjoying.

As time passed, I started reading different versions of the Bible. I was scared, but I knew I was so lost and empty. I was brought up on the King James version, and as beautiful as it is I really didn't understand so many parts of it. I started reading the New Revised version and this time my reading was becoming clearer. It was as if light bulbs were lighting up the dark areas of my mind and heart. Jesus was actually revealing His Word to me. I was a baby in Christ, *Matthew 11:25-27, "At that time Jesus said, "I praise You Father, Lord*

I knew because of that small voice in my heart, that the Lord was revealing himself to me. The road to the cross of Christ was not an overnight journey for me. It took awhile, in fact, years. Did I backslide? Yes. Did I still wonder about how saved I was? Yes. Was I a little bit saved or a bunch saved?

That tends to be one of the games Satan will play with your mind. If you should go there, remember saved is saved, and sin is sin. One thing I did realize, I could never again fully turn my back on the Lord. I wanted to do things my way. I went against His will for my life so many times. But then I didn't know what His will for my life was. I still didn't know how much Jesus loved me, or even understand why He would love me. I didn't see just how precious His patience with me was. Though my heart cried out for God, in my mind I was condemned.

Satan attempts to condemn us with every sin we commit, the Holy Spirit inside us, which is the presence of Jesus, the power of God living in us to lead us to repentance and life. **Romans 8:1 "Therefore there is NO**

*CONDEMNATION **for those who are in Christ Jesus…"** When I acknowledged my need, my sins, my faith in Jesus Christ I became 'In Christ Jesus.' So do each of us who sincerely make this confession. I was finding that through everything, testing from God, temptations from Satan (there is a difference), there has been challenge, peace within myself, unbelievable joy, rest and most of all, victory. Unlike Jesus, there was and is plenty of sin in my life before I came to the cross and even now.

Sin has to first; be acknowledged and, second; dealt with through repentance, asking forgiveness and making amends, repaying. I also found I had to forgive others for the pain they caused me.

WHAT? THOSE WHO HURT ME NEED TO ASK ME TO BE FORGIVEN, I CAN'T DO THAT, I CANT FORGIVE THEM FOR ALL THE HURT THEY CAUSED ME, FOR STEALING MY INNOCENCE, FOR PUTTING ME THROUGH PAIN NO CHILD SHOULD HAVE TO GO THROUGH. THERE'S JUST NO WAY. I CAN'T AND I WON'T. My mind could not comprehend that this would even be possible. But as I learned and accepted the love of Christ for me, I struggled long and hard with love your enemies. Let me tell you, **THIS WASN'T EASY!!** I didn't know it at the time but hate and unforgiveness were eating away at my insides. They disturbed my sleep and kept my stomach upset. They slowed down the process of my spiritual growth. Time and energy was being wasted on getting even and the uselessness of reliving my past. Psalm 37:1 says, ***"Do not fret because of evil men or be***

envious of those doing wrong." Even the time I spent just wishing, that they would get what was coming to them, could have been so much better spent elsewhere on something positive.

Only the Lord could help me through this, I couldn't do it on my own, didn't want to do it at all. But, I found out that **as I forgave, I became free**. The stony, hard places in my heart for each person who did me wrong and used me, ceased to exist. As time went on, whenever I thought of a person who hurt me, I thought of them as a child of God; a messed up creation of God who needed God's love, God's forgiveness, God's guidance in their lives just like I needed God in mine. My grandmother used to say, you can't keep praying for someone and hate them at the same time – prayer will win out. I learned this. It's still not easy, but it's true.

One of the things that helped me get through this time of learning to forgive was a scripture, which I came by accidentally, *Matthew 6:14,15, "For if you forgive men when they sin against you, your Heavenly Father will also forgive you. BUT if you DO NOT FORGIVE men their sins, your Heavenly Father WILL NOT FORGIVE YOUR SINS."*

Friends, this was not just for back then. This scripture still is not just a good suggestion for us to do, this is <u>**an emphatic commandment, it is a promise.**</u> If we forgive, we will be forgiven. If we do not forgive, we will not be forgiven. Tough,

rough, and sometimes bordering on the
impossible, it can and must be done. We each
have a destiny, and as long as we keep un-
forgiveness in our lives, we cannot fully be
prepared to fulfill what God created us to
do. With unforgiveness we will never reach
our full potential in Christ Jesus.

JESUS OUR EXAMPLE

The greatest example of forgiveness came from Jesus who had no sin. He was condemned for who He claimed to be, not for anything that He did. He presented as a threat to those who were used to being powerful, listened to. Those who did not understand the heart of Jesus were threatened by His love.

He was beaten to where His flesh hung from His skin. He was unrecognizable. Beaten because men were insecure in their positions. We still persecute who or what we don't understand. Jesus was beaten, ridiculed, nailed to a cross, hanging, bleeding and suffocating; not for one thing He did wrong. Jesus loved us from the beginning of time, and He showed His love. Genesis 1:27, ***"So God created man in His own image, in the image of God He created him; male and female He created them."***

John 1:1-5, ***"In the beginning was the Word, and the Word was with God, and the Word was God. He was with God in the beginning. Through Him all things were made; without Him nothing was made that has been made. In Him was life, and that life was the light of men. The light shines in the darkness, but the darkness has not understood it."***

Jesus was publicly ridiculed and rejected as the Son of God. Did He fight back, or attempt to get even (as we would have)? Did He curse those who wanted Him dead? Did He reject those who rejected Him?

NO! NO! NO! At the end He said, "Father, forgive them, for they know not what they do."

Why did Jesus, who was without sin, allow himself to go through all that pain? It sure wasn't that He liked pain. As a man in the flesh, Jesus didn't want these things to happen. Jesus knew what He was in for, He knew from the beginning of time what His end would be, and still He chose to die this death. John 10:17,18, ***"Therefore does my Father love me, because I lay down my life, that I may take it up again. No man takes it from me, but I lay it down of myself. I have the power to lay it down, and I have power to take it up again. This commandment have I received from my Father. Matthew 26:39 states, "Going a little farther, He fell with His face to the ground and prayed," "My Father, if it is possible, may this cup be taken from me. Yet not as I will, but as you will."*** Wow, every time I read that I feel the power of His act for us. But you say, He was the Son of God, He could do that. NO!! His physical body operated just as ours does. He felt pain just as we do. What made the difference?

LOVE AND OBEDIENCE: He said often, John 12:49, ***"For I did not speak of my own accord, but the Father who sent me commanded me what to say and how to say it,"*** Jesus demonstration of love for His Father, recognition of who His father was and what His father's plan for mankind was **LOVE IN ACTION**. Love from the Father meant that God would sacrifice His **ONLY** Son for us. John 3:16-18, says ***"For God so loved the world that He gave His one and only Son, that whosoever believes on Him shall not perish but have eternal life. For God did not send His Son into the world to condemn the world, but to save the world through Him. Whoever believes in Him is not condemned, but whoever does not believe stands condemned already, because he has not believed in the name of God's one and only Son."*** God knew that without His love we would continue in our sinful ways and completely miss the blessing of knowing who He is, His love for us, and we would miss being with Him, forever.

In order for me to forgive, I needed the example of Jesus love for us and of God our Father, I needed to see His forgiveness of ignorant, sinful men who preyed on those they thought weaker or different than themselves. I needed to see my sins, and know that God forgives me still, and that I don't have the right to live in un-forgiveness of others and call myself a follower of Jesus Christ.

The only thing that could restore us to God and bring salvation to man was a blood sacrifice, the blood of Jesus Christ, God's only begotten Son. Jesus was born of a woman, Luke 1:31, **_"You will be with child and give birth to a son, and you are to give him the name of Jesus…"_**Jesus was conceived by the Holy Spirit of God. This is the same Holy Spirit that breathed life into Adam at the time of creation. Genesis 2:7, **_"And the LORD God formed man from the dust of the ground and breathed into his nostrils the breath of life; and man became a living soul_** (KJV). This breath was free from sin, a holy bloodline created by God. Jesus was the second Adam, created without sin in His bloodline, but born of a woman, subject to human frailties created by God.

Jesus lived His life according to His Father's will. (This is exactly what God wanted from Adam) and gained victory over all sin, even victory over death, Jesus did this for us, you and me. He did this because of love for us. But Adam, unlike Jesus gave into sin. Sin took us away from God; **Jesus brought and bought us back.**

Father, forgive them. Father, forgive us. Your will, not mine. I don't know how often I have had to say these words or how often you will. But I guarantee you if they become a part of your everyday vocabulary, you will start to experience a peace within yourself that you never knew before. Sometimes you may not feel very forgiving. But be for real with yourself and God, because He knows what we're feeling anyway. Admit it, **"Even though I'm not feeling very forgiving, I know I need to forgive, help me Lord to be forgiving."**

SELF-RECOGNITION

No I haven't left the foot of the cross yet, this is still just the approach. It wasn't easy to get to the foot of the cross, or to stay there once I got there. I had to see the blood He shed for me; I began to realize the pain He suffered at just the thought of bearing the sins of the world in His body.

I had to examine myself. What do I feel when I am wrong. When I do something evil and know it, what goes through me? GUILT, SHAME, CONVICTION, FEAR. Can you imagine what it was like for Jesus to take all that upon Himself? He took the sin of man that came before Him physically upon the earth and the sin that was present, and the sin of every future generation which includes us and those to come. In His body He paid the penalty of sin for us. He closed the gap between us and God our Father. He was the one and only blood sacrifice that had to be paid from that day on.

I saw Jesus on the cross. I saw myself as helping to put Him there. Though the cross was His purpose, every sin I committed help put Him there, aided in His pain.

Have you ever thought, "I'm not that bad, I don't mistreat people, I'm honest, I try to live a good life? In my own eyes my sins weren't that despicable, I thought I tried to stop being the devil's child, and was pretty good most of the time. I now see that my actions or non-action helped to pierce Him. My drunkenness, violence, gossip, fornication which I took part in, and sometimes (quiet as it was kept) initiated; allowing someone else's dirt to invade my ears and my spirit were some of the things that helped to wound Him. I helped to wound him with my own selfishness. When I failed to give a kind word, a smile, a helping hand, a kind thought, a prayer. Just being with people who were doing wrong was giving an approval, so I sinned at times by association. I was helping to wound Him with my sense of pride in who and what I was.

What do you see of yourself at the foot of the cross? Get the picture?

Mark 7:21-23 reads, ***"For from within, out of men's hearts come evil thoughts, sexual immorality, theft, murder, adultery, greed, malice, deceit, lewdness, envy, slander, arrogance and folly. All these evils come from inside and make a man unclean."*** Which of these things do we all carry in our hearts? Can we acknowledge our guilt, repent and give it up to the Lord? **WE MUST.**

I'm sure there were people in the crowd and members of the Sanhedrin who did not cry for Jesus to be crucified, but they didn't cry for His release either. I'm sure there were those present when He was being beaten that cried for Him, that realized the injustice of the whole thing, but they didn't try to stop it. I know there were people in the crowd who did not believe

Jesus should be put through a shameful crucifixion, but they didn't try to stop that either. There have been many and will be many more times when I've been found guilty. How about you? But Jesus continues to reach out to us, and shows His love for us.

I know now, I could have done nothing to stop the suffering of Jesus during that time. It was for that purpose that He came to cover our sins with His blood. His destiny was to pay the price of our sin that we might live for eternity with Him in heaven. Does that excuse us from sin today? **NO!** If and when I commit sin, I know I'm guilty. But I take comfort when I read in the Word, **John 1:9** says, ***"If we confess our sins, he is faithful and just and will forgive our sins and purify us from all unrighteousness."*** So as He forgives me, it leaves me with no excuse to not forgive others.

WHO IS JESUS IN MY LIFE

Jesus died for us. Jesus paid the price to redeem us and His blood cleanses and washes away all traces of our sin. Only through His shed blood can God, our Father look at us and see what He really created us to be. I realized that Jesus did not just die, but that He still lives.

After Jesus died a horrific death for us, He did something so glorious that there is and never will be a comparison to it – **HE ROSE AGAIN FROM THE DEAD.** Jesus is alive and well, and it was witnessed by many who walked with Him, talked with Him, ate meals with Him, and who examined the holes in His hands, feet and side.

Jesus lives and He's with God advocating for us, pointing out His chosen people to God. Jesus is alive and lives in us through His Spirit. We are the temple of the living God. For **Jesus said, "I and my Father are one."** Satan is still trying to claim our lives and says, "Yeah, but Jay did this and Jay did said that…, Satan tries to condemn us." But the Bible says in **Acts 13:39,** *Through Him everyone who believes is justified from everything you could not be justified from by the law of Moses."*

At the cross Jesus forgives you and me, and He asks that His Father forgives us too. At the cross we start all over again, **CLEAN.** Because we're clean we can see things in a new perspective. We can see, feel and hear love through the love that Jesus showed to us on the cross. Still at the cross, I realize that part of my purpose is to know the love, power and authority of Jesus. Not just know about Him and what's in it for me, but **KNOW** Him; have a relationship with Him. I never realized that it was possible to have a relationship with Jesus.

Revelation 2:4, *"Yet I hold this against you: You have forsaken your first love,"* talks about leaving our first love. We should always make Jesus our first love. We should always remember what we were, where we have been, what He has brought us out of, where we are going, and who will always be there for us. Jesus is my reminder that who I was without Him, I am not the same person with Him. Jesus reminds me that the direction my life is now taking is totally different.

Someone once said, "The things that it took to get your love, it will take that and more to keep your love." I can't neglect Him and expect to remain close to Him. When it feels like He's no longer with me, I do a life check. Is Christ trying to work something out in me? Is this a test of faithfulness, or have I been slipping back into past behaviors? What's He trying to say to me? I go to His Word and I pray, then I have to be still enough to listen for His answers.

Think about close friends. We are aware of each others likes and dislikes. We know the kind of people we like to be around. We know what will bring a smile to our friend's faces or what will make them frown. It's the same way in forming a relationship with the Lord. We learn who this person is and what He's about. I realize now that everything I went through was **NOT** God's will for my life. His perfect will for me, for us is good. His purpose for us is good. Man makes the choice to serve God in goodness, or the choice to live apart from God in sin.

There were times in my life when I said, "Why God, why me?" As I grew older I said, "If there is a God He wouldn't let this happen to me." I said, "There is no God, I'm my own God." Oh, that was really dumb to say. Sometime The Lord will give us a taste of what we ask for. This was one of those times I experienced all kinds of things happen to me that were out of my control, but by my own independent choices. I had car accidents, people coming into my life that shouldn't have been, and I was momentarily attracted to them, I was exposed to lifestyles I never knew existed, and I knew how to cry out for God and ask Please forgive me, take me back. My life was in a state where I couldn't see Him. I couldn't feel Him. All I could see was trouble and evil around me, my own actions included. Some of the things that happen to us when we are separated from God have long lasting and devastating effects. Just because I acknowledged the Lord, and he forgave me, didn't mean that I did not have to pay the consequences for my decisions during that time.

I didn't fully realize before my request for independence from God, that the evil, devilish acts which were committed against me and millions of children were not His will. I began to see they were man's choice to sin. I was beginning to realize that the root of our problems are not so much racial, political, sexual or in our genes. The root of our problem is sin and separation from God. Reality says sin will touch each one of us in some form. **Romans 6: 1-2**, reads, ***"What shall we say then then?" Shall we go on sinning so that grace may increase? By no means! We died to sin; how can we live in it any longer?*** I was dying a spiritual, eternal death and didn't even know it.

Who is Jesus in my life? He's my Lord. He has ownership of me. Who is Jesus in my life? He's my Savior. I know that in times of trouble He is there for me. Who is Jesus in my Life? He's my friend. In prayer I can talk to Him like no other. Who is Jesus in my life? He is my Comforter. There are many times when I can actually feel His warmth and love surrounding me, giving me that peace beyond all understanding. Who is Jesus in my Life? He is the one who re-introduced me to God, our Father as one of His chosen ones. Who is Jesus in my life today? He is my provider of all good and perfect gifts. He is my guide who will **NEVER** lead me astray or leave me alone. God cannot and will not accept sin. Jesus paid the price for our sins then, now, and forever. The choice to accept Him, His love, and His freedom is ours.

LOVE COSTS

As I looked at my children who were so innocent, I realized they were entrusted to my care for my teaching. I thought I would never hurt them or allow anything bad to happen to them (so I thought). I would never intentionally choose to put them in situations where they could get hurt. These were my children, my only true and innocent loves. But when we live apart from God, bad things happen to good people, even innocent people, even my children. My children witnessed many, many mess-up, sins in their mom's life. I do realize how blessed I am to still have their love and respect.

Because of the path I chose for my life I neglected some major areas of their lives. Then I couldn't see I was hurting them. I worked; they had food, and decent places to stay. I learned the hard way there is more to being a responsible parent than just providing for the basic need. I said earlier the days are gone when a parent can say, "Do as I say not as I do." Eventually our children are going to experiment in the same things they see us doing. I praise God they have grown into healthy, successful adults who are making wise choices for their lives. Several followed briefly the path I took, but being smarter than I (Yes!!) didn't stay on the downward slide long. They were there just long enough to learn down isn't where they were called to be.

The times I missed in their lives can never be brought back. The things they saw in me can never be removed from their memory. I live with that. I also live with their forgiveness and love. As they grow in their parenting, at times I can point out something they are doing that was exactly as I did to them, then we can talk about the effects it had on them as children. When things are out in the open it is so much easier to stop the continuance of negative, damaging actions from one generation to the next.

One of the major things I have learned is that we are not born loving. Remember I said earlier, I thought when I became pregnant that I would have someone to love me. I found out that from the beginning of life, it's about getting our needs met. A baby cries when they're hungry, wet or in pain. They learn that as they express their needs, others meet their need – or not. They mimic our expressions and our actions. Love is either learned and put into action or not learned, and selfishness takes over. When self takes over we have a whole new breed of other horrors to deal with; and none of them will lead to honor or respect.

Ask yourself, how you would feel if your children or someone else you loved were forced to love you? Love is to be freely given. Love is a choice. We are obedient because we respect, and respect is earned – but it's still a choice. Would you be satisfied with mandated love? Is there such a thing as mandated love, or would it just be acting the part? Would you desire just a show of respect without a commitment and the feeling of honor and love? Forced love or respect is not true, it's nothing that can be valued or trusted. I don't want a false show of love or respect. Feelings like that must come freely from the heart. Isn't it great when people make a choice to love you on their own? Isn't it great when your children make conscious efforts to obey you? It's wonderful when your friends know what please you and they do it, just because.

I bet God feels the same way. He doesn't force us to do anything. I believe that would be a very empty victory for God or anyone else. God gave us a free will to love Him, and obey Him. Yes, there are commandments and expectations, but nothing that works against us. Everything God has done and set before us has been for our benefit. We have laws of the land that we must obey (maybe we fudge on a few), some man-made laws work against us. But God's law always works for our good. Take some time sometimes and seriously read and study through Leviticus. You will see the human benefits that God had in mind to protect us from poor health, disease, family, neighborhood and community conflicts. The commandments that God gave Moses, man couldn't keep. And they weren't enough to save us from ourselves, or our choice of sins. Then came Jesus. Jesus came to lead us back to God. When He was asked, what's the greatest commandment? He replied, **"Love the Lord your God with all your heart and with all your soul and with all your mind. This is the first and greatest**… But hold on, He said, ***"the second is like it: Love your neighbor as yourself."* Matthew 22:37-39.** When we keep these commandments, we will keep the others. None of the commandments work against themselves, but toward our good.

Look what has happened in the last 25 years, a generation. Look at the difference of how we react about God. Look at our society, and how the value of human life and moral ethics has decayed over the years.

I said in the beginning, it's all about love. At the cross, I realized that love wouldn't happen without Jesus in my life. Love wouldn't happen just from reading the Bible without understanding or doing what it says, **James 1:22, *"Do not merely listen to the word, and so deceive yourselves. Do what it says."***

I'm not saying don't read the Bible. It's through the Word of God that we come to understand who God is and what our purpose in this life is all about. Through reading the Bible and praying, we begin to see our relationship with Jesus; we begin to understand the likes and dislikes of Jesus. Through the Word we see what He requires of His followers, what makes Jesus angry and what makes Him happy.
There is a cost to everything we do.

THE CROSS

The cross where Jesus died,
I didn't know Him
He shed His blood for me,
I cared not for Him
I saw the cross, His wounded body draped
How was I to blame for this?
I played no part.
What did He want from me?

They say He came to set the captives free;
To heal the brokenhearted;
To forgive our sins.
He came to do this mighty thing for me,
I never cried for Him - Until
Thru' my tears
I saw the spear, my sins
I saw His blood on my own hand.

By, © J. L. Johnson
1997, rev. 2005

At the cross I realized love wouldn't
happen just by telling people they are loved
by God. Love takes action. That came to me
one day while I was downtown. People were
passing out tracts and telling these
homeless, hungry people that God loves them.
How? Where is He? There was a church in
Seattle that met downtown (rain or snow)
every fourth Saturday to feed the homeless
or anyone who wanted to eat. Other churches
took turns on different weekends. By
mingling, talking, sharing experiences, food

and clothing, by laughing, and holding their babies, and sometimes crying with them, we could pray and introduce or re-introduce Jesus. **We must meet the needs** of others. Sometimes we can identify things that we were not given earlier in our lives, but as we have come to know Christ and receive His love, we give as we receive (materially, spiritually and emotionally).

At the cross we experience the true cleansing love of God. God gave to us what we must give to others. For some this may be the first time you can say, "Someone really loves me, someone really sees me for who I am, and loves me anyway; someone sees my needs and loves me, **loves me.**"

For me it was really difficult after so many years of abuse and four unsuccessful marriages to truly say Lord I trust You. It was difficult to really mean it. One of the good things I learned through this whole process has been not to act out of fear.

It was almost next to impossible for me to say Your will, not mine. This was partly because God is masculine, and also because I couldn't see Him. Giving over my will to God was one of the most difficult steps I had to take as a Christian. The Bible says if we cannot love our neighbors (mankind) who we can see, how can we say we love (and trust) God whom we have never seen? Think about it.

I spent years blaming God for my bad decisions. Now I had come to a point where I openly acknowledged that it was not God, but

me who made the choices. In all my marriages
there was one common denominator – me. I
made choices without thought to consequences
for myself or anyone else. I made choices
based on what I wanted right then, or
thought I needed right then. I made choices
out of fear. Our past defiantly can
influence our decisions, our future. But we
cannot be blind to facts about people and
things we want to do that will have a
negative or deadly, in some cases, impact on
our lives. There were warnings from family,
friends, and circumstances I ignored. What
price love? or was it lust?

It hurt and it was scary to realize I
could no longer blame my family, past abuse
or God. It also freed me to begin to make
decisions based on facts and the Word of
God, instead of feelings. I made a choice
for abusive relationships. I made a choice
to live in the fast lane. I made a choice to
hang with unstable, not trustworthy people.
I was warned. I ignored all advice. I made
the choices. Remember when I wanted to be
removed from God, I said "I am my own God."
It was during this time that I entered into
a relationship which was almost deadly. It
was only God's power that delivered me. God
protected my children and He allowed my
family and true friends to stand by me
through the whole ordeal of becoming free.

I don't believe God intended for any of
us to stay in physically dangerous
situations. Some of you too may be going
through something that seems to have no good
end. **God can deliver, please trust Him to**

show you the way out. He never fails. When some of you think about trusting God, it may be the first time you begin to think of a man as being able to show **PURE LOVE**. For some it may be the first time you're able to put your trust in anyone at all. At the cross we begin to learn and to trust.

We may not have received all the love and nurturing that we needed. Once we experience the love that Jesus gave from the cross, then we are able to live in peace as children growing in God. When we accept and experience the Love of Jesus we can pass on to others a new love, friendship and kinship in Jesus. Through our own individual, unique experiences we can let others know that because of what Jesus did on the cross, we are whole. We have sound minds because of Jesus. We love people because He loves us. We love God and Jesus His Son.

HEALING TIME

It took awhile but I now know how to love and respect myself, no matter what happens to me. I am a creation of God with purpose. I am special. In Psalm 118:17 the psalmist says, ***"I will not die but live, and will proclaim the works of the LORD."*** What are the works of the LORD? **I AM and so are YOU.** Did you know that? You are the work of the Lord, created to live an abundant and full life; created to love and to be loved. We are created to give and to receive.

Looking back over my life has never been easy. The first time I really took a look at me, I was in my late twenties and working with a counselor about the abuse issues. She had me write about my early childhood. Later in my late thirties, I did this process again. This time I took into account marriages, me as a parent, and relationships. This I did so I could see the pattern my life was taking with the decisions that I made. All of my chosen relationships were co-dependent in some form. I chose relationships where I thought I would get more out of than I could give. I depended on the other person to make me whole, valuable, and happy. I was still feeling more comfortable with known authoritative, abusive personalities as partners. It was hard to break away from something I had grown comfortable with, even though it was detrimental. I was looking for someone to take care of me, make my decisions, someone to blame when things didn't go right.

The third time I wrote about my life was the most special and truthful time. This time it was done with and through the leading of the Holy Spirit. I was more dependent on the Lord than I had ever been. I was living in Mississippi, completely away from my supporters and at times my enablers; family and friends.

I knew Christ was using me to touch the lives of women who were going through so many of the same abuses I had experienced. Once again, study time was on. I answered a challenge by a TV minister, Jack Hayford, and made a commitment to start my day earlier by spending at least one hour a day in the Word, and more time in prayer. Not time in prayer asking for things, but for the Lord to really speak to me, to lead me. At some point in all this one hour turned into two, and if it was my day off and I was alone, the time could easily pass to three or four hours. Wow, this was amazing; that I could spend that much time in the Word, and it seemed like so little had passed.

It was during this time of prayer and study I realized that Jesus had been with me my whole life. I just hadn't really looked for Him. I had haphazardly asked Him into my life, God's not stupid. He looked past my faults, saw my need and came into my life. He does know when we're serious. Until then I hadn't fully realized or appreciated that it was He who saved my life - several times, many times. Not counting several suicide

attempts, God would not let me die. There is
a song that says, "If Jesus has to reach way
down, Jesus will pick you up." Well He
reached way, way down, saved my soul from
damnation, and picked me up from life's
gutter more times than I can actually count.
This last time I wrote about my life
something else happened. I was able to renew
my commitment to Him. I learned that I
needed the covering of the Lord over my life
EVERYDAY. It was not enough to wait for a
revival, or a profound revelation that I
needed to recommit. I now recommit my life
to Him daily. Daily I seek Him and His will
to be done in my life, and give to Him my
life to use.

    I call my time in Mississippi my desert
experience. Though I had a young daughter,
acquaintances and some friends, I was alone,
except for God. In Mississippi I realized
that in everything I had been through, I was
no different than millions of women. What
abuses I experienced, so had others and so
will others still. I learned I was a child
of God, in His family and so are they. God
freed me from sin, depression and low self
worth. What He did for me, He has done, and
will do for others – all who call upon Him.
He loves us so much that He gave to us
Jesus, His Son. John 3:16

    Facing **THE CROSS** in Mississippi, I
began to be healed spiritually, emotionally,
and physically. Healing begins through
Jesus, and His healing is available to
everyone who asks. Healing in any form will
mean new growth. The process of healing

often hurts before the wound is healed. Healing is another step off the baby food of pabulum and milk before we can eat more of the solid foods of faith. Like a baby we start a growing period of learning and experiencing this new life in Christ Jesus. Be sure, Satan has not forgotten us, and he will attack us. He'll use every temptation where we are weak. He will even use people close to us to get us to separate from Jesus. With every step we take toward healing, wholeness and getting closer to the Lord, Satan will be there to taunt us, to try to pull us back like white on rice.

During the healing process we learn how to live whole. What does that mean? What does wholeness look like, when our lives have been filled with chaos? For me learning to live whole meant having confidence in making decisions. It meant learning to live alone. After another divorce, could I learn to be 'okay', content, confident in myself? **OH YEAH**, I was able to see and appreciate all the talent God had blessed me with. It wasn't easy, and I cried many tears for a few years. Sometimes still do. But that's okay too. I know God has a plan and a purpose for my life.

It was during this process that I had to learn how to pick my associates. Many people who have been abused are often way too trusting. Wanting to be accepted we haven't always learned a very important word, 'Boundaries.' In 2 Timothy 3:1-7 Paul talks about people we will meet, and how women (gullible, silly) women can be easily led off. When I read this it really touched home. Did you know men could also be affected like this? As humans, there is a need to be wanted, to be loved. If we have not discovered who we are we can easily fall victim to the users of this world.

For years I tried to do right, but I NEVER came into the knowledge of who I was in Jesus. I never really understood that it was not me who chose Him, but Jesus chose me. John. 15:16, You did not choose me, but I chose you and appointed you to go and bear fruit-fruit that will last. Then the Father will give you whatever you ask in my name.

Romans 8:28-31, **"And we know that in all things God works for the good of those who love Him, and are called according to His purpose. For those God foreknew He also predestined to be conformed to the likeness of His Son, Jesus, that He might be the firstborn among many brothers. And those He predestined, He also called; those He called, He also justified; those He justified, He also glorified. What, then shall we say in response to this? If God be for us, who can be against us**?"

Jesus chose us, and there has been a purpose for our lives since before the foundations of the world. We, you and I are created to conform to the image of Jesus Christ. What better image could we have?

I said in the beginning of this book. No matter who you are, what you have done. God loves you, and has a perfectly good plan for your life. Thank God, I FINALLY can see and accept this.

I was learning to live whole. I found my desire to spend weekends partying or drinking beginning to dwindle. If I did have a drink, I could drink one instead of the whole bottle. I drank what I wanted in moderation. I didn't need it. When you get rid of a habit, you must replace it or it is so easy to return to the same old patterns. My time was being taken up with more productive things. I became more involved with community, the church. I went back to drawing. Learning how to live whole meant depending on the Lord for finances instead of men. It was a new way of life, but the Lord always came through for me, and my children.

When we live healed we don't have the constant attention we had, when we were unable to do for ourselves. We learn to stop living in the 'ME', and more for others. When we are healed we also have to learn how to live with people who have thought of themselves, or even became our 'caretakers.' Now they have to learn how to allow us to wean ourselves from their care. It can really be difficult, especially if these people have an authoritative (controlling) personality. When we are healed we even learn to live with people who may have mistreated us.

Becoming a healed, whole person is a rough process. It may be you need help along the way. If you need counseling – **GET IT.**

     There are Christian counselors. I
advise you to seek out a qualified person
who will assist you spiritually, and who is
able to guide you through all the emotions
you will expend during this process.

<u>**WHO DO YOU THINK YOU ARE, OR WANT TO BE?**</u>

I was in my thirties before I even started figuring that one out. By the time I was thirty years old, I had been through three marriages, and had made several suicide attempts. The Bible says God hates divorce so naturally I thought He hated me.

I was still all wrapped up in trying to please others, and finding my worth in what other people (men) thought about me. I was so blinded that I didn't recognize what it was taking to raise four boys and hold down two jobs. I could see no good in my life, except for my kids. And I thought they were too good to have me for a mom. At one point I packed a small suitcase and was ready to leave – to abandon my children. I was just going to disappear. I knew they would be better off without me in their lives. My Mom often helped me financially, as best she could. I was ashamed of always being in need. I thought my family would take care of them, better than I could, and definitely they would give them better values than I could. Not once did I consider the burden I would be placing on them. Not once did I consider what abandonment would mean to the kids, or how it would affect their growth, their future, their parenting in years to come.

I remember my thirtieth birthday. Oh I got calls from my mom, grandmother, aunts, cousins and a few friends wanting to party, and all wishing me a happy birthday. My kids had a birthday party for me. After they went to bed, I was alone in my bedroom. Well almost alone, a fifth of Crown Royal was with me. I had been getting real close to the Crown for a couple of years. That night I spent drinking, crying and looking in the mirror at the wretched thing staring back at me. I cried because I couldn't provide for my four sons. I cried because I was useless. I cried because I was tired of working two jobs and not having anything to show for it. I cried because I shoulda' been a better mom, a better person, a better everything. Really, I had one fantastically bad **PITY PARTY**.

As I looked in the mirror, over and over that night I asked my self, "**WHO ARE YOU**?" There were no positives that I could hear in my head all night. My whole life up to that point seemed like one gigantic screw up after another. The answer to who I was always came out to equal **NEGATIVE – NOTHING – ZERO**.

In my drunkenness and self-pity on my 30th birthday, this is what I heard. Who are you Jay? *Uneducated, slow to learn, dumb, nothing.* Who are you? *Someone who's always broke.* Who are you? *Stupid, don't even know how to balance your checkbook, handle your bills, or keep enough money to maintain.* Who are you? *Unlovable and alone, nobody wants you.* Who are you? *A loser. Who wants a loser but another loser?* Who are you? *You are the ugliest person in Seattle. Ugly! ugly, ugly.*

*Look at yourself, you're big, your nose is
too big, your hair is too short, and you
have no personality.* Who are you? *A thing,
used up and wiped out, sexually and
emotionally. I'm not even a good mother.*

     I felt dead, but as usual I was
miserably unsuccessful at dying too. In my
mind, <u>my drunken mind,</u> I heard all night
long (even while I slept), **You're a failure,
failure, failure – You're NOTHING, YOU WILL
ALWAYS BE NOTHING!!!**

     Satan was seriously trying to take me
out, and I was falling for it in a big-time
way. Everything we do has a payoff. What did
I get out of my night of self-pity? Two
swollen eyes that I couldn't even open, and
a missed day at work too. **HAPPY BIRTHDAY TO
ME!**

     I have included a picture of myself at
that time in the back of the book, so people
can really see how Satan plays with your
mind. The picture I had of myself was
nothing like what others saw.

     During the years between my twenty-
eighth and thirty-fifth birthdays, I was
unsuccessful three times at suicide
attempts. Twice I tried with pills, and once
I cut both my wrists (at 59, I still carry
the physical scars). On the wrists episode I
was on a three month leave of absence from
work (a very high-paying responsible
position); close to a nervous breakdown;
drinking way too much; and behind in my
house payments(blessed to have built a

house). I was so scared of losing everything I'd worked for, everything my family had helped me to build for my children. I was so afraid that everyone would finally really see what a failure I really was. I was trying to find an escape, and using every (unfounded) excuse I could find to run – to get out of responsibility.

I know there are people who will read this who can relate to running. Running away isn't the answer even to a short term solution, let alone provides for no permanent solution. Suicide, whether by drugs or your own hand serves no purpose; it only hurts badly those who you say you love. It destroys the wonderful purpose God had for you and me when He created us.

I was even active in church and still hurting. I was trying to live a double life. Serving God on Sunday mornings, singing in the choir, taking my kids to church. Then at home sinking into the Crown Royal or Jack Daniel bottle. I had at twenty-nine begun a relationship that lasted almost seven years. Remember the one I said was almost deadly. Fear of being alone often stopped me from making smart choices. This relationship was physically and emotionally dangerous in every sense of the word. I was scared to leave, scared to stay – wishin' and hopin' he would change. He did, for the worse. I did too, for the weaker.

There were several in my church family who knew what I was going through, and tried to pull me out of the fire; I wouldn't

listen - I wasn't ready. I shut the door on
so many positive relationships. What I was
going through wasn't any of their business
anyway. Through my actions, I sank deeper
and deeper into depression. I wouldn't cook
or clean, I was to the point I really didn't
want to bathe. Death had to be better than
this. I was tired, just tired of existing.
That pity thing had returned big time.

One thing I learned is that blues
songs, alcohol, pills and problems never go
together. I remember clearly sitting in the
blood filled bathtub of hot water, listening
to a "She don't have nobody song."

After my thirtieth birthday I realized
I had to make some changes, and I did. I
went back to school. Flunked out three
times, and it is during one of these times
of flunking out that I tried to commit
suicide for the last time.

I was in the bathtub, drunk and slicing
my wrists. What I couldn't do in class I was
doing in the bathtub - counting and naming
the layers of tissue under my skin. I was so
full of booze, even today as I type this I
can't remember the physical pain, but I cry
for that emotional baby who was sitting
naked in a tub of hot water. I cry now for
that woman who had no sense of the greatness
the Lord had called her to. I cry now for
the millions of women and men who haven't
found their way to the Lord or out of their
mess. I don't remember calling for help, but
I do remember waking in the ambulance, and
again waking the next morning in the
psychiatric ward of the hospital. They kept

me overnight, and released me with just what
I needed - a whole bunch of pills to relax
me till I could see the doctor. One bit of
advice they gave me that did help was to
See an attorney about not losing my house.

The same day I was released from the
hospital my mom came from Minnesota to be
with me for a while. My sons had called her.
They were so strong to put up with me
through all those years. I had hurt them so
much and even then didn't really know how
much.

My mom and I did a lot of talking and
praying, praying and talking - something we
really needed to do. My grandmother is an
evangelist, pianist and singer. She made me
the most beautiful, encouraging tape. To
this day, every time I play it, I know that
my relationship with God was deepened. One
song in particular, "If you can just hold
out until tomorrow, everything will be
alright," is still one of my favorites.
Now, today I can honestly say and believe;
THIS TOO SHALL PASS.

Several days later, I still had
bandages on my wrists, I looked in the phone
book, and found the name of an attorney, Mr.
Joseph Barraca. I wore a blue sweater with
very long sleeves to cover the bandages; a
small part of the bandages could still be
seen. Mr. Barraca greeted me, and went
behind his desk and sat down. For a few very
long, awkward moments he didn't say
anything. He just looked at me. It wasn't a

look of pity or disdain, or condemnation. It was a sorrowful look, like he could see into my soul, as though he too felt my pain. I felt like shrinking. I was ashamed. After a few minutes Mr. Barraca asked, "Are you a Christian?" Well that did it, I sat there and cried for I don't know how long, and he fed me Kleenex after Kleenex. He also gave me a small New Testament, and told me to carry it with me everywhere I went. Then he led me to 2 Timothy 1:7, **"For God has not given us the spirit of fear, but of power, love and a sound mind."** With the help of Mr. Barraca, I kept my house (Single ladies, make sure you homestead your house if you're buying).

Once again I was drawn back to the Lord. When we accept the Lord into our lives, He not only has chosen us, but has a plan for our lives already sketched out. We are in His hand and we cannot be snatched out of His hands or His Father's, **John 10:28, 29.** The Spirit of God has always drawn me back to Jesus. I'm so glad that He **NEVER** gave up on me, even when I tried hard to shut Him out of my life. Through prayer and reading His Word, God again began revealing more of Himself to me. But, all was not yet well – at least not in the natural.

Satan does not like to lose, and I believed he thought he had me all the way this time. After my mom left, I started watching the 700 Club in the mornings (never did like those TV preachers). But I really hungered for an understanding of the Word.

The mother of my then daughter-in-law started visiting me. We prayed together even when I didn't want her there. We studied the Bible together. She made me write a list of all the people who would be affected if I should succeed one day at killing myself. She hung it on the wall right in front of my bed, where I could see it everyday when I woke up. Slowly, I was beginning to believe that I was lovable and that maybe God could love me too.

It was a terrible thing I did to my kids. Many times they walked on eggshells so I wouldn't get upset. As a parent I often would find something wrong in what they were doing, and that would be my excuse for a major attitude. I am so sorry for what I put them through. My kids (not prejudiced at all) are the best and smartest that I've ever known. I thank God that none of them were as messed up as I was at their age, or at any point of their lives. Were they perfect? No. But considering who their mom was, they turned out great.

All was still not altogether well for me, or my soul. As I was finding out who Christ was in my life, strange things were beginning to happen. The house where we lived was one that I was able to have built by God's grace. Anyway, I started feeling very nervous, afraid in my own home. It was like I wasn't alone there when I was supposed to be by myself. It was not a peaceful presence. My two oldest sons had moved out, but my two youngest children were still at home. They didn't seem to notice

anything. I asked my neighbors if anyone had
died in the previous house that was there,
but they replied no. I couldn't figure out
what was happening to me. My friends asked
if I was still taking the pills I came home
with. Well, I wasn't. They made me feel so
out of control, and kept me sleepy and still
depressed.

One night I was lying in my bed, but
while I was still very much awake, there was
a tremendous presence in my room. My bedroom
door was open and the light from the living
room could be seen. Suddenly, my room became
pitch black; blacker than anything I've ever
experienced, an empty blackness of no
shadows. I was scared, and I felt a
heaviness that was all around me and on me.
I couldn't move. I was it seemed frozen in
one spot. I couldn't scream. All that could
come out of my mouth was a gurgle of sorts.
I felt helpless. This was a terror I had
never known before. I began choking like
something was trying to enter my throat. I
knew it was evil, and I could not stop it. I
wish I could say that the name of Jesus came
immediately to mind, but it didn't, I was
struggling in my mind. But suddenly (praise
God for the suddenly times) when the thought
of calling the name of Jesus came to me, I
still couldn't say His name. It was a
struggle, but I knew with all that was in me
I had to claim Jesus, both in my mouth and
in my heart. I had to call His name as
forcefully as I could. I knew that if this
thing entered me, I would be lost. Somehow I
knew then and know to this day that the
power to say the Name of Jesus came from
Him. Jesus had claimed me already and I

screamed, **JESUS! JESUS!** Whatever it was, this demon thing left me and has never returned. As soon as I spoke the name of Jesus I could again see my surroundings, and felt my strength return. One thing I know is that the life I have lived Jesus has watched over me.

I have lived around abusive people and been around the drug scene. I've been diagnosed as a week-end alcoholic, but on that night I don't know what my life would have turned into. I've asked for cocaine and acid and people selling it wouldn't even sell it to me. I've had bartenders tell me to go home, because I didn't belong there.

God has a way of protecting us even from ourselves. Take a few minutes to think back on the people you may have encountered with eyes that could cut you thorough, empty eyes with nothing in them but hate. Oh, thank You Lord for your grace.

I have only told a few people about this encounter, and I really think they thought I was crazy or just they didn't believe me. I even started to doubt myself until recently (1997) I heard a preacher on Trinity Broadcasting Network (TBN) Benny Hinn, tell of a similar situation. I sat straight up, in awe of the confirmation. All I could do was sit there and cry – I knew it was real. Others have had this experience. Satan is real and he attacks, but JESUS had chosen me. I was, I am, and **I'LL ALWAYS BE HIS.**

Remember my thirtieth birthday, when I asked the question of Who are you Jay? Well, it was several years, and about approximately six months after I cut my wrists when I asked myself again, Who are you Jay? This time I could see there were positive opportunities and realistic answers for the present, and my future. **Who are you?** I am someone who can make much out of little. I'm still short on cash, sometimes. I need a higher paying less stressful job, so I can be home more with my kids. **I GOT IT!**

Who are you? I am someone who takes a little longer to learn things, especially if they have to do with numbers, but once I get it - I've got it. I give my best and get the promotions.

Who are you? Physically I'm not the ugliest thing I imagined in my mind. Alcohol and drugs actually do change a person's appearance, and it's not for the good. I am, no matter what I look like, created in the image of God! Strangers take pictures of me, I've modeled (another story) I'm always being complimented about my dress.

One year later - **Who are you Jay?** I am a woman still in an impossible relationship. I am a woman who is able to ask questions about the value of this relationship. I certainly am not unloved. I've been looking for "love" in all the wrong places, for the wrong reasons, and with the wrong people. **LOVE BEGINS WITH ME.** One of the things Jesus said is to love your neighbors as you love yourself. I have to learn to love me first. I started doing things again like reading, and renewed an old love - drawing, I even joined a bowling league. That put me with more positive thinking people. I could go for walks alone and appreciate the beauty around me, and appreciate my own thoughts. I take care of me, long, hot, smell good bubble baths, and concentrated on my nails, ankles, heels, eyes - all that stuff, just for me. I get stronger, knowing Christ is making a difference in me, the way I think, the way I act and the way I look.

Three years later - **Who are you Jay?** I still have too little education, but I went back to school. After cutting my wrists I went back to school, flunked again. Then another student gave me some invaluable help on study techniques. God is so good and so are people. I went back and quit because of funds. I was on welfare for awhile, and my mom paid my tuition, but when welfare found out they cut my check, and I had to repay the amount of the tuition back to them - extra income. A church member was Vice President of Honeywell, Inc. in Ballard, and helped me to get on there. I returned to school, and Honeywell paid part of my tuition as long as I maintained a "C" average. This time I made it, I was on the Deans list (A's Baby!). I took two classes at a time, worked a full time job, and was still raising my kids. But I learned I wasn't stupid. Can you imagine what those "A's and B" did for my ego? **Who are you Jay?** Definitely not used up emotionally or sexually. It took a lot of years and a lot of help to get it into my heart and my mind that I wasn't really responsible for what happened to me as a child. What I wasn't responsible for as a child, I don't have to carry around or hang onto as an adult.

If you have had a similar childhood of sexual abuse issues to deal with – know for sure, God can and will deal with those who have abused you. Whether you are a man or woman You can overcome! With the grace of God, I am daily becoming a new creation!! Everyday is filled with possibilities. Sometimes I still say, **"Okay Jay, who are you becoming?"** One thing I know for certain, **I AM NO LONGER THE VICTIM, through the grace and mercy of God I am Victorious.** Jesus is the ultimate healer.

Assessing life is a process that does not end; it must not end. Who you were or are at 5, 15, 25, or 50 does not apply to who you are going to be in years to come. All of our experiences from childhood through adult-hood, help to make us who we are today, but our circumstances do not have to limit who we will be tomorrow.

WHO IS SATAN LOOKING FOR?

One thing for sure Satan wants to keep us in a victim mentality. ***1 Peter 5:6-10, tells us that Satan is searching for whom he may devour*** (eat up, take away from God). Remember the song from the 60's "Searchin'?" When we're living without God, we're in Satan's control. We're always searchin' – complete satisfaction never comes to us without God. But when we come to the knowledge that we need the Lord and accept Jesus as our Savior, acknowledging Him as God's Son – automatically, we get on Satan's hit list. Now it's his turn to search, and he will always be searching for our weaknesses and ways he thinks he can separate us from God.

If you really want an adventure, excitement, risk, get on the Lord's side. There is nothing boring when you live a Christian life. This will be a time of extreme testing. Who are you, what do you really believe, are you willing to walk in the things you talk about? Where are you going, and who are you going with? In chapter 5 of 1 Peter, verses 6-8 they tell us what we can do, and who Satan is looking for.

Verse 6, Be Humble: Satan is looking for those who are proud, still seeing themselves and their accomplishments as number one (1). Above all Satan can use those <u>who will not</u> humble themselves before God, His will, or the knowledge that comes from the Word.

Verse 7, Cast Your Cares On Him: Whatever is bothering us give it over to the Lord. Let Him fight your battles. Satan is always looking for those who are going to solve their own problems without God. Don't need to look to God for anything, us independent, proud types. In **John 15:5,** Jesus says, "...without me you can do nothing."

Verse 8, Be Sober: Satan is looking for those who have little or no self-control in their appetites (food, drink, drugs, men/women – as the song says, "Different strokes for different folks"). Get it under control – you ARE Being Watched and Pursued. **BE VIGILANT:** Satan is looking for those who are sleepwalking with their eyes wide open. He's looking for those walking around unaware that danger surrounds them. He's looking for those who are not watchful or comprehending of the situations or the people around them, even in our families.

If you've made Jesus Lord of your life, and your family, friends, lovers, etc. have not, **BE WATCHFUL.** Your new love for Christ will not be understood, and may not be accepted by those who have yet to know Him. Their interest may not be for the good of your eternal soul or your life. When you start developing your time with God through His Word and through prayer, you start moving out of the victim mode into victorious living.

At the cross, we not only see Jesus as a sacrifice for our sins, but Jesus comes with His alive self to comfort us, and shows us what victory looks like. Because He is victorious, we are victorious. Because He has new life, our lives are new in Him. We are created to become the image of Jesus, oh yeah, that's **VICTORY!**

Satan is looking for each of us to look back with regrets with mixed emotions. He plays mind games with us about how much fun we had out there drinkin', snortin, and shootin' it up. He tries to make us think that the chaos and confusion in our lives was excitement. Oh, but God can give you excitement, where you don't have to worry about the police coming to raid your house or take your kids. God can give you laughter that will last, and you don't have to pick yourself up from the toilet bowl where you've vomited all over the place and ruined your new clothes. Jesus can give a glow on your countenance that will make people notice, and question where have you been, and who have you been with. Satan wants us to think we are helpless, but the Word of God says, **"Greater is He that is in us than he that is in the world."**

WHAT'S YOUR CHALLENGE?

What situations have you gone through that when you really stop to think about it, it might be considered a miracle that you still have a sound mind, or that you are still even alive. Have there been events in your life that hurt you, which you had no control over? Maybe you were young, or maybe you were afraid for yourself or someone else. Maybe there seemed to be no alternatives for you. If this is the case, and you're still reading, you may be feeling uncomfortable.

Because you are here, you are alive today; you are a survivor, and more importantly – **A WINNER.** God's plan for our lives is more than just surviving. He calls for His children to live abundantly. It takes more than money or position to make a person a winner. It takes courage to live, courage to get through one day at a time – sometimes we must and can only make it one hour at a time. It takes courage to say **"I WILL LIVE."** Not just inhale and wait to exhale, but live. It takes courage to decide to use your bad experiences to help yourself. It takes courage to use your own experiences to help others through their experiences. **IT TAKES COURAGE.**

TODAY

One day, perfection when our eyes will cry
no more.
But for today, we shed tears from eyes
Too old - yet young

One day, perfection when at peace our minds
shall be.
But for today we pray, renew our minds with
Thoughts of You, oh Lord, today.

One day, perfection when Your face, dear
Lord we'll see.
But for today, we seek Your face, Your love,
Your will
In all we say and do - Today

By,
J.L. Johnson © 1997

Just because you live and breathe you
will be thrown some hard curves along the
way. **You can make it**! I did, and you are
just as much a child of God as I am. The
good news of Jesus is that He came that we
all might be free from **<u>all</u>** those things that
hold us back, and will eventually destroy
us. Jesus came to break the hold that

depression has on us. He came to set us free from your experiences of physical, emotional and sexual abuse so you can function as a whole person. Jesus came to break the hold of witchcraft, future and fortune-tellers. Did you know Jesus knew and knows our future? He's waiting for us to acknowledge Him in our lives. Our future is in His hands, and He tells us *"it is for good and not evil," **Jeremiah 29:11**.* Jesus came to break the hold that drugs and alcohol have over our lives. Jesus came to stop the backbiting, gossiping, lying tongues. Jesus came that we would be free to live – to have victory over everything that Satan would try to throw at us. **Jesus came that we would see Him for who He is. He is the precious Son of the living God who holds all power in His hands.**

What's your challenge? Does any of this apply to you? If so, what will you do about it? Think about it. You've read this far, and I know that the reading is evoking a whole lot of memories in some of you. But you're still reading. While you are reading, you're working through some issues, or at least identifying some that things need to be dealt with – **THIS TAKES COURAGE.**

Always remember, you are **SPECIAL, UNIQUE, ONE OF A KIND.** Though your situation may be similar to someone else's – There is only one of you. You **CANNOT** be re-created, and your being, your presence **CANNOT** be undone. Even those who have committed suicide have made an impact in this world on someone else, and that impact cannot be undone. Dying may seem like the only answer to a painful life, but really it's not.

Jesus has the answer, and He is the answer. Jesus said, "I am the way, the truth, and the life…, John 14:6. You want answers, go to His Word. Allow Jesus to reveal Himself to you. Allow Him to love you. He does and will continue to love you.

Some of you are still living with too much pain in your lives. Some of you are feeling as if there is no way out, and you know the despair of not wanting to live another day. You've tried so many things. You've tried the "How To Books." You have been baptized in almost every religion under the sun. Some of you have tried to live without "religion". Some of you have tried work, sex, alcohol, and drugs - you've tried everything but Jesus. **Try Him, He Won't Fail You.**

I remember when I was going through a time when I chose not to believe in Jesus (early 30's). I felt like I had done everything preachers and teachers and books had told me to do, and I still was no farther than when I had begun. I thought I had to be perfect to be accepted. I thought I had to give up smoking, drinking, cursin' and sex. I wasn't ready for all that, and as often as I tried - I failed. I didn't realize that all I had to do was come, with a willing heart to follow Jesus. I didn't realize that Jesus does the cleaning up, As I learned from Him, about Him, and wanted my life to be in Him, I did not want all those worldly things in my life. Eventually I didn't curse as much. I had an ongoing battle with cigarettes, wow – now that's a story; a miracle.

I was attending church and Rev. Kenneth Ransfer pastor of Greater Mt. Baker Baptist Church in Seattle, stopped me one night after prayer meeting. He told me the Lord had showed him that I was a teacher. Well, this was a confirmation that I had been struggling with (he didn't know it). From my home training, I knew if I were going to be in a leadership position I could not cause others to stumble. Okay, **I LOVED CIGARETTES,** the taste, the smell, and the way they made me feel. I was a grant writer, and I could smoke and write all night. Smoking, I felt helped me get my thoughts together. Dilemma: give up what I **REALLY** liked, or not do what I knew and had been confirmed that I was to do.

I don't believe no one is going to hell because they smoke, but we are accountable for what we do with and put into this body. If Jesus is my king, the power in my life; can I allow this small piece of paper and tobacco to have command over my life? What message does this send to others? In the Bible Paul talks about if what he does causes someone else to stumble, then he needs to quit. I've tried so many times to quit because it was affecting my health. WELLLLLLL, I got on my knees, and asked God to take the taste away from me, and the desire. I asked Him to allow me to be around it without feeling the need to have one, because in my work I was around people who smoked. I threw away a carton, washed out my car, washed the walls, sent my clothes to

the cleaners, and stayed away from my smoking friends for a week. I also had a large 4x4 ft. canvas and started drawing the crucifixion. I haven't had a cigarette since. Praise God! Trust Him to handle your addictions. I had been smoking since I was 13 years old till I was 50, now at this writing I'll be 60 in October 2005 and still smoke free without a yearning.

Women, men, young and old – if your sexual hormones are active, and you think you cannot contain yourself without the benefit of marriage – that's a lie. Because we are who we are, temptations will come, but JESUS makes a way out of temptation for us. When we turn everything over to Him, He can take those natural desires away. You can be victorious in all situations. Okay the question, what if I fall and go back? Don't let Satan beat you up. GET UP! Ask for forgiveness. Don't use your freedom in Christ of forgiveness as an excuse to sin. But give it to Him who makes you strong, and counts you as faultless because His blood covers the sin that you've committed and Satan stands as your accuser.

It is Jesus who will make a difference in our lives where we cannot. he has left us the power of His Holy Spirit who lives within each of us who confess Jesus as our Savior. **Philippians 4:13** reads, *"I can do all things through Christ who gives me strength."* In **Ephesians 3:16** the Word says, *"I pray that out of His glorious riches he may strengthen you with power through His*

Spirit in your inner being…; verse 19, "…

and to know this love that surpasses knowledge—that you may be filled to the measure of all the fullness of God".

Abuse in any form, whether it's done to you or you do it to someone else or you abuse your own body takes away from who you really are. Abuse provides, for some of us, several identities to cling to. I'm not talking multiple personalities. I'm talking about the innocent child who gets locked inside, and the street-smart person who protects the child. Most people see the street-smart part of us, the one who has learned to fight, use others and ourselves to get what we want, and some of what we think we need. But as much as we try we cannot fully protect that child who is locked away. Year after year as the abuse continues the child begins to die.

Like an alcoholic recovering, when you shed the negatives, drugs, hurts, despair, depression, etc. you reveal or expose the child you left behind. That child at its last innocent emotional age is still there waiting to come out and play, waiting to trust, waiting to live. But the child is scared to reach out in fear that someone else is waiting to hurt them, take advantage of them, or use them. Jesus is waiting for the child to come out, He's waiting to grow you and love you.

Our walk with the Lord is a faith walk; a challenge of trust. Jesus will not let you go. That's not to say we won't have disappointments again, we will. Life happens, and we learn to deal with life with Christ leading the way. There is in each one of us the "nice" girl or the "responsible" boy who wants to be "respected" for who they are. When the child goes into hiding because they feel dirty, used, or susceptible to a new hurt, only a select few can see the innocence inside. Your pain is so deep that the only way and time you can forget about it is when you're stoned out completely. **CHALLENGE:** To acknowledge your powerlessness day by day, be open honest and willing to see and live life in a new way. **CHALLENGE:** To accept that others care about you, and allow them to start seeing the child. When this happens growth happens. Few have known the pain you've felt, few know the genius it took for you to survive, few have seen the tears you shed when you've been hurt, or the tears you shed when you've returned the pain on someone else. Does anyone really care? The cycle of hurting can end.

No matter what you do, good, bad or indifferent, you have made an impact in this world. **CHALLENGE:** To live. Your life will not go without remembrance from someone. Some people think that suicide is an act of selfishness. Usually people try to kill themselves out of the fear of living, tired of being hurt or hurting others. I believe it is an act of misplaced understanding. People haven't learned how to love enough to live.

At the cross Jesus died to this physical life. He became a willing sacrifice for each of us, taking onto Himself every sin that was, is, and ever will be committed. He gave His life that we could live, and be found right, clean and sinless in Him through His shed blood. Jesus knew every sin we would commit yet He loves us. Jesus felt the pain of every one of us that has been hurt. He did the work, He paid the cost - we just have to accept that He is.

At the cross is the beginning of life. Our realization and acceptance of Jesus as our Savior brings on a new birth in us. We become **BRAND NEW** Creatures. We are the same old physical us's; our feet still hurt, and our corns and bunions haven't disappeared. But we are reborn into a spiritual family, God is our Father; God the Son, Jesus our Savior; God the Holy Spirit, our helper, and He lives in us leading and guiding us in the ways of Jesus.

How many times have you wished to start over again? **This is the time**. We are offered a new life instead of throwing away a life. Each one who is reading this does matter to someone. Living allows each of us an opportunity to see what a difference can be made. There are people who love you and don't know how to show it. The answer for your life is at the cross. Jesus is the answer. Repent of your sins (be willing to turn your back, give it up). We have tried and tried to clean ourselves up. And keep on falling back. Only Jesus can do the work on us. If we are willing to admit we can't, and that we need Him - He will. Jesus died for us. He arose from the grave for us to live and start anew. He was seen by over 500 people. And the testimony of those who saw Jesus has stood for over 2,000 years. Jesus has commissioned us to life.

CHALLENGE: To ignore the voices that tell you, you aren't good enough, you will never be accepted, worthwhile or lovable. Satan will still try to tempt you. Hold on to Jesus one more day, then another, and another. Choose to see the challenge of life through to the end with Jesus, your Savior, your Friend, your Comforter, your Guide, and Lord of your life.

I WILL YET LIVE

When I'm all alone,
And no one is near to me,
When my pain is unbearable,
And no one wipes my tears,
That's when a still, small voice inside says
—
You will yet live!

Life sometimes seems hopeless,
And gray skies never shine.
Reminders of my past are present at all
times.
That's when the Holy Spirit says,
It is for you Jesus died, You will yet live.

I will yet live to praise Your name.
I will yet live, Your works You will declare
in me.
I am Your handiwork it seems,
The creation of Your hands,
Praise God, Praise God, Praise God,
I will yet live!

By J.L. Johnson 1997 ©

VICTORIES

I've had many victories in this growing process. I will continue to grow in the Lord.

- It is a victory to see my children grown with families of their own.
- It is a victory the relationship that I share with my mom and grandmother.
- It is a victory to be able to continue drawing, painting, jewelry making, writing, and making Mama Jay's Hot & Spicy BBQ Sauce.
- It is a victory that God has allowed me to touch so many lives in Mississippi, Washington, and wherever this and my other books and poetry go.
- It is a victory that I can stand on the street each week, and wherever I am and declare that Jesus is Lord.
- It is a victory to stand and say that Satan has not destroyed what God has purposed for His use - ME.
- It is a victory to choose to rejoice and be glad in the day that God has made.
- It is a victory that God has put business opportunities in front of me.
- It is a victory that on October 20, 2007 I became a licensed minister of the Church of God, Anderson Indiana in Washington state.
- It is a victory that I can stand and say, "I will not be defeated; for God I will live, for God I will die."

I hope you will make the journey to the cross, and take time to stay there and let God heal you, and love you, but remember after the cross came the RESURRECTION - NEW LIFE.

No, It won't be easy. No, it's not fun working through the stuff. Yes, memories of years gone by will flood in and probably cause tears to flow. But remember with tears comes release. With every victory (and you will have victories), you will discover just how pure, precious, and strong you really are. With every victory you will know that you are not alone. With every victory you will have more love to share with others.

In Revelation 12:10-11, it says that **"...*Satan, the accuser of our brethren is cast down by the Blood of the Lamb (Jesus) and by the word of their testimony; and they loved not their own lives unto death.*"** Our life is for eternity with Jesus Christ.

This book is just one woman's story. I pray to read yours one day. There is Victory in Jesus, and with every victory you can say, **"WITH THE GRACE OF GOD, I MADE IT."**

Because you live and you've allowed Jesus to live in you, there will always be unfinished business, unfinished work until He says, **"Welcome Home My Good and Faithful Servant."**

AT THE CROSS IS JUST
THE BEGINNING OF LIVING!

Made in the USA
Monee, IL
07 July 2026